To Nick, Angie, and Gary.
— M.B.
To Bob, editor extraordinaire.
— G.B.

The Best Alphabet Book in the Wild West

TEXT BY GARY AND MADELINE BENNETT

ILLUSTRATIONS BY GARY BENNETT

Featuring LetterBug

And the Buffalo Bug Band

There are hidden letters in this book
Ranging from A to Z.
If you have trouble finding some of them
Just follow the tips from me.

Bubba

Buster

Billy-Bob

and Paul

The illustrations were created with Adobe Illustrator.
The text was set in Futura Book, bold, and extra bold.

Designed by Gary Bennett
Edited by Bob Early

Prepared by the Book Division of *Arizona Highways*® magazine, a monthly
publication of the Arizona Department of Transportation.

Publisher — Nina M. La France
Managing Editor — Bob Albano
Associate Editor — Evelyn Howell
Art Director — Mary Winkelman Velgos
Production Director — Cindy Mackey

Printed in Hong Kong.
Library of Congress Catalog Card Number: 99-63521
ISBN 0-916179-96-6

Aa
Armadillo

Arnie Armadillo remembered he was from Amarillo, but couldn't remember why he was at the Alamo. Maybe Davey Cricket can help.

A hidden "A" is very, very near. Do you think it might be by Arnie's ear?

2

Bb
Buffalo

Buffie Buffalo and the Buffalo Bug Band love to sing and play mooosic.
They could boogie all night long singing their ABC song.

There's a letter "B" hidden up high. Why don't you ask the butterfly?

3

Coyote

Carl Cowboy and Carla Cow are carefully cooking carrots and corn over a campfire. They love vegetables almost as much as they love the call of the coyote.

Now that you've seen this page, and had a chuckle, you might look for the "C" in the cowboy's belt buckle.

4

Dd
Dinosaur

Dexter Dinosaur's most unfavorite thing is being dragged by Dainty Doris through the dusty desert to their daily dress-up party.

Look for the letter "D" cleverly hidden somewhere; it could be on a cactus, or it might not be there.

Ee

Elf owl

When it snows in the desert, Elvie and Eddie Elf Owl enjoy getting decked out
in balls and holly to catch snowflakes for breakfast.

To find a hidden "E" don't make a mistake. Look up high at a big snowflake.

6

Ff

Fox

Little Fara, the Fire-fighting Fox, is frustrated by fire started foolishly in the forest.

The letter "F" is hidden in Fara's fur. But you'll have to look closely to find it on her.

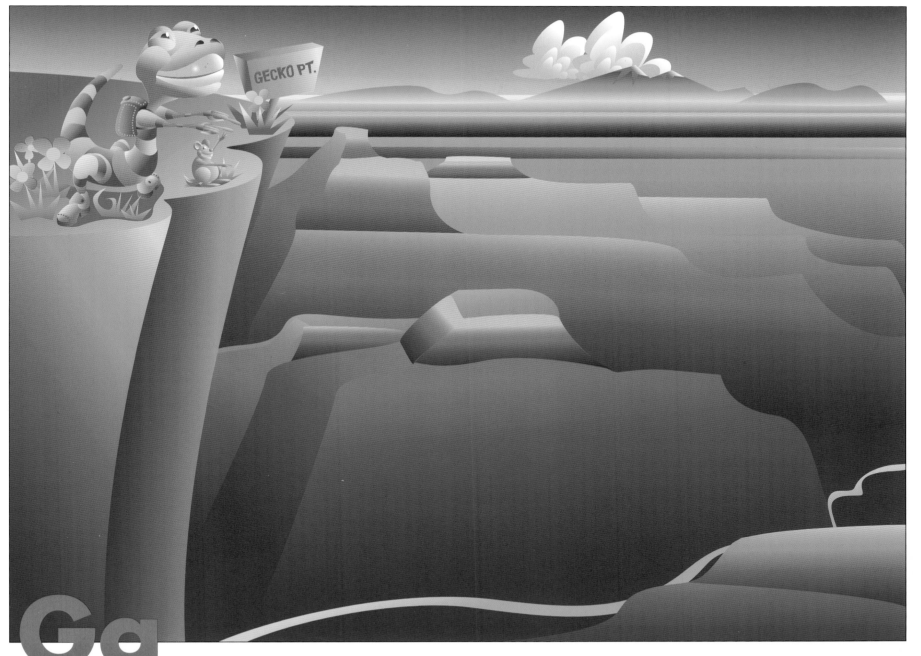

Gg
Gecko

The Grand Canyon always makes Gilbert Gecko gasp, grin, point,
and say things like, "Golly," "Great," "Gorgeous" and "Grab my hand."

In this picture is a hidden letter "G". Maybe the grass is where it could be.

8

Hh

Horned toad Halloween is Hector Horned Toad's favorite holiday. He likes to hide, pop out of a pumpkin and yell, "Hello," except, when the lid is stuck, he calls out, "Help."

 "H" is the letter to look for now. It's probably hidden on the pumpkin somehow.

Ii

Ibis

Iris Ibis is such a cool bird. Instead of flying south for the winter, she ice skates, eats ice cream and makes figure eights.

Iris likes to draw on ice. She drew an "i" just once, not twice.

Jj

Jackalope

Jack-a-lope, Jack-a-lope jump so high, Jack-a-lope, Jack-a-lope touch the sky, Jack-a-lope, Jack-a-lope you like it hot. Tell me if you're real or if you're not.

Are there horns in this picture that look like a "J"? Somehow Jaclyn knew you would see it that way.

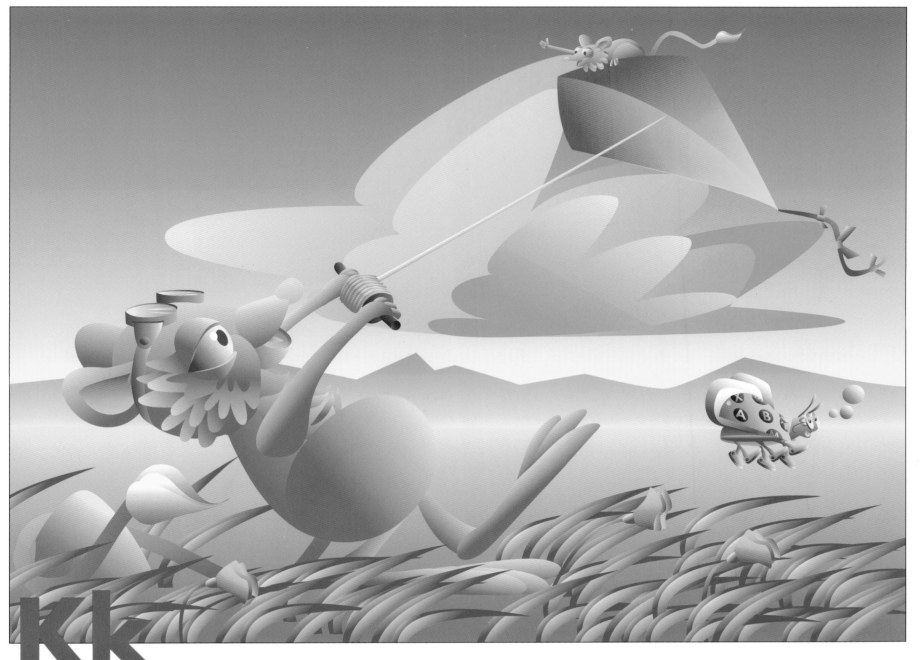

Kk

Kangaroo rat

Keith Kangaroo Rat has found the key to kite flying. It takes a keen kite, a kind breeze and a friend with a kindred spirit.

 Can a kite fly without a tail? The letter "K" might help it sail.

12

Lizard

Lois and Lester Lizard love to lounge in their life jackets, but little Leon prefers leaping from a ledge into Lake Powell.

Is that the letter "L" floating by? It's there, you'll see, if you give it a try.

Mm
Mountain lion

Maddy Mountain Lion loves mountain biking through Monument Valley. She is thinking how massive, how monumental, how marvelous, but mostly -- how tiring.

Try looking at the flag, you never can tell. If the letter "M" is there, it's hidden very well.

14

Nn
Newt

Little Nathan Newt is usually nice. Except on bath night when his nice nature becomes nasty. He screams, "Not again, never, no way." But then, "OK, as long as there's no next time."

If you haven't been successful, I won't let you fail. To find the hidden "N", just look at the tail.

Ocelot

Oscar Ocelot gets lost a lot, especially among the ocotillos. Perhaps he needs a compass. Ocotillos look alike a lot and that confuses poor Oscar Ocelot.

After tying his boot lace in a great big "O", Oscar decides which way he should go.

16

Pp

Peccary

Pigcasso Peccary is a polite artist. He always says, "Please" and "Thank you" and sometimes, "Pardon me while I paint the Petrified Forest and Painted Desert."

If a painting peccary hid the letter "P", the artist's canvas is where it should be.

Qq

Quail

When Quincy Quail sits reading in his secret, quiet place, he's so happy even a quizzical LetterBug can't make him quit.

If you were going to hide letter "Q", do you think you'd put it on Quincy's shoe?

Rr
Roadrunner

Rhonda Roadrunner would rather rollerblade than run,
but rabbit and rattlesnake prefer to rest and read.

The letter "R", you surely should know, is neatly hidden by rabbit's big toe.

Ss

Snake

Simon Snake masters the skateboard using a seat belt for safety, while Silvester Snail slides under the shade of Sunset Crater.

There's an "S" in this picture, part animal, part plant. Some people see it, but others just can't.

20

Tortoise The only place for a tough little Tortoise like Tommy is Tombstone, the Wild West's toughest town. So Tommy and his trusty trike "Tooter" hit the trail; that is, if it's OK with Tommy's mommy.

Is that a "T" in Tommy's star? Then this is the easiest letter so far.

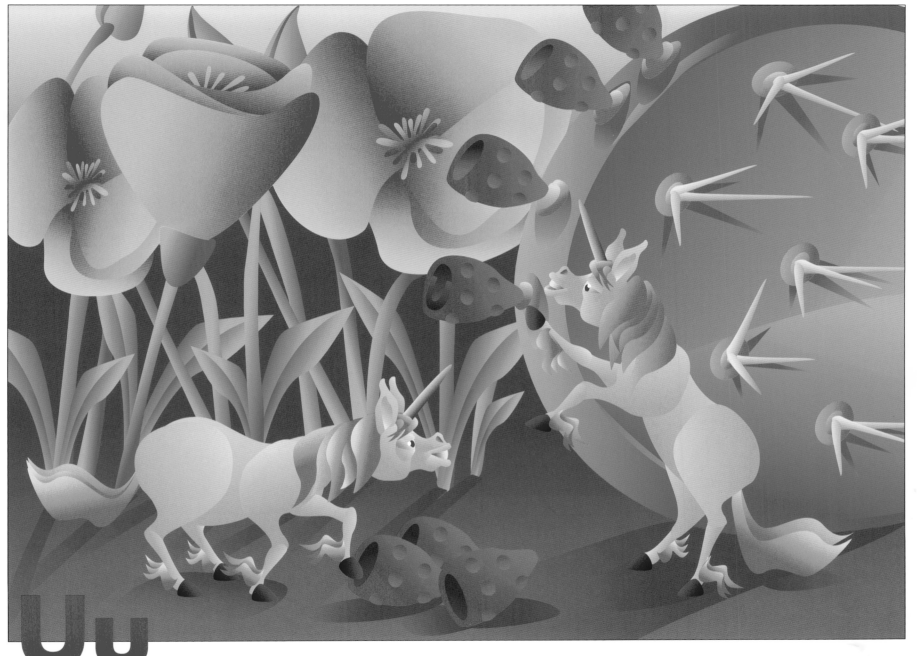

Uu
Unicorn

Undetected, unseen, and under cover of desert wild flowers, tiny Ursula and Ulysses Unicorn come out of hiding to gather prickly pear fruit.

As Unicorns gather fruit in the sun, one finds a "U". Can you see which one?

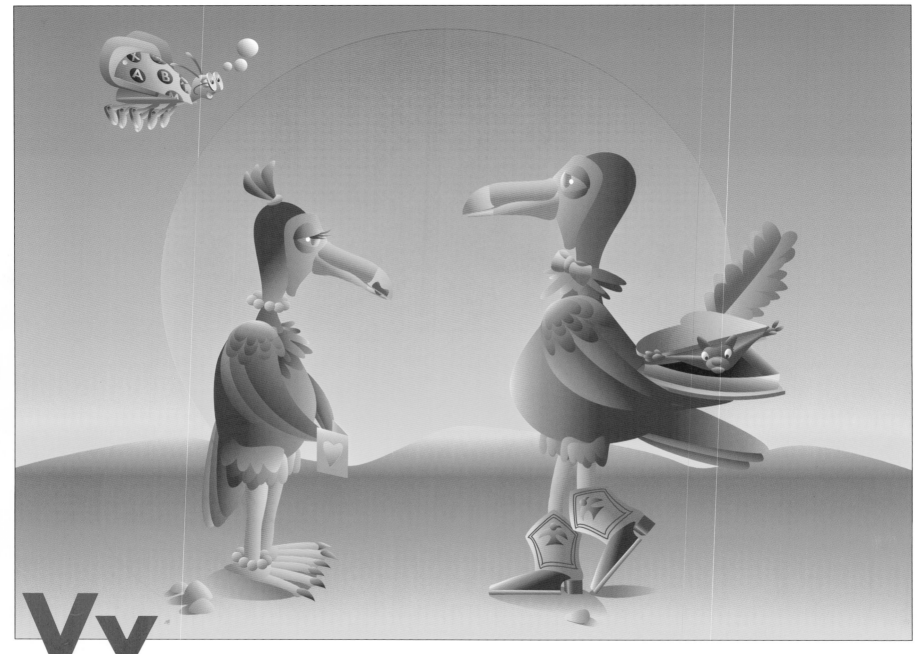

Vv

Vulture

Valerie and Vinnie Vulture love to exchange gifts on Valentine's Day. Valerie likes to read verse to Vinnie, and Vinnie sometimes brings a cute varment to Valerie.

 Someone here that you can see holds up his fingers to form a "V".

Ww

Wildcat

Wilbur Wildcat wants to be a wrangler. He wrestles cows, wears cowboy boots and watches John Wayne movies to perfect his Western walk.

You will find the letter "W" in a very likely place. It's where a cowboy brands his horse, and it won't be on his face.

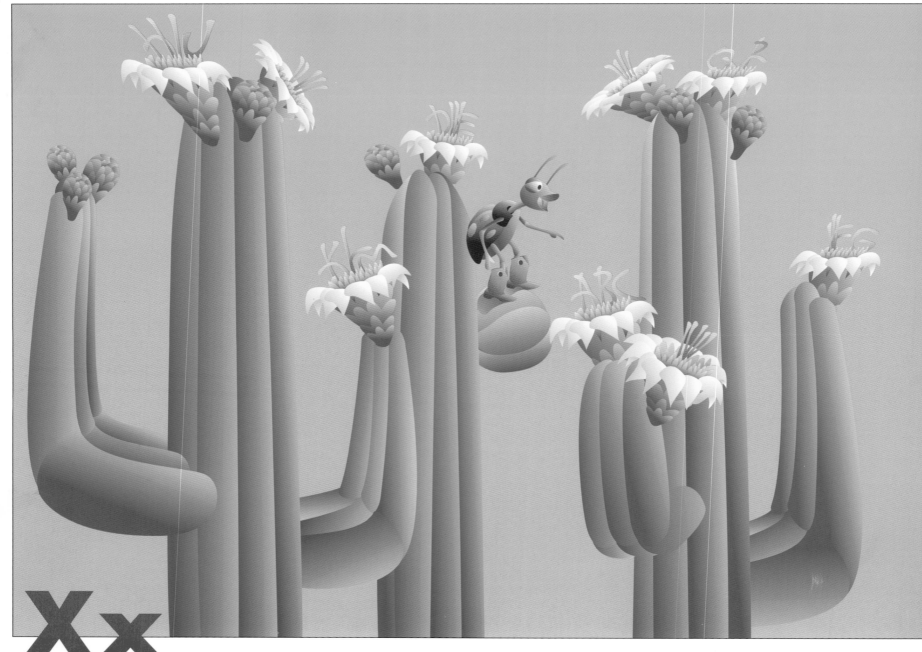

24

Xx
X marks LetterBug's secret reading spot

Can you find all the letters from "A" To "Z"?
They lead to LetterBug's secret reading spot and beyond.

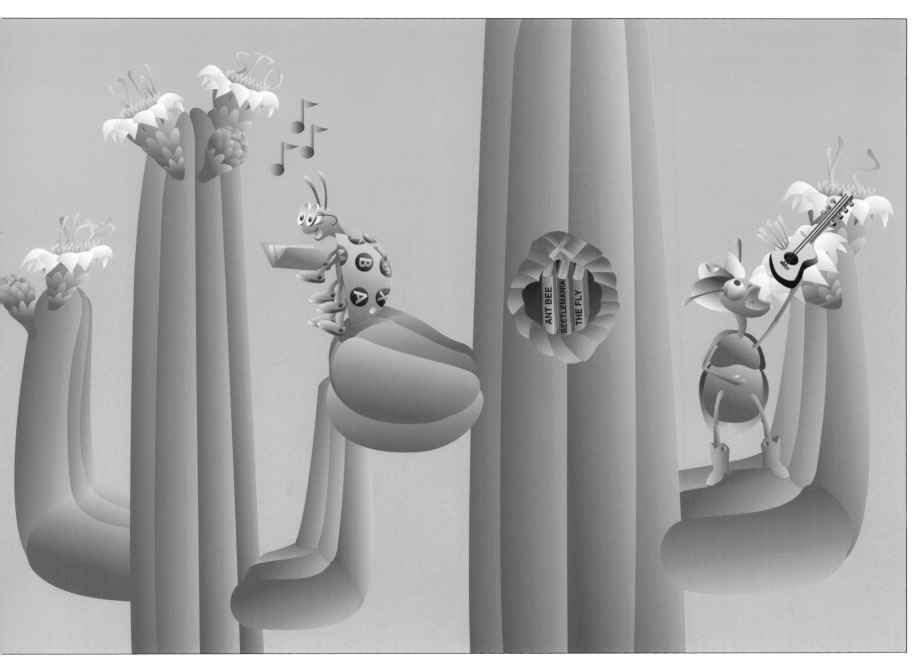

 Buster will show the way by pointing out the letter "A".
Bubba will let you see the final letters "Y" and "Z".

Yy

**Yellow
warbler**

"Yippie ki yo, Yippie ki yea." The song of Yancy the Yellow Warbler can be heard across Yellowstone Park. Some say, "Isn't that nice." Some say, "Isn't that loud." Others just say, "Yuk, isn't that enough?"

You're as smart as the LetterBug and even wiser. Use your skill to find a "Y" erupting from the geyser.

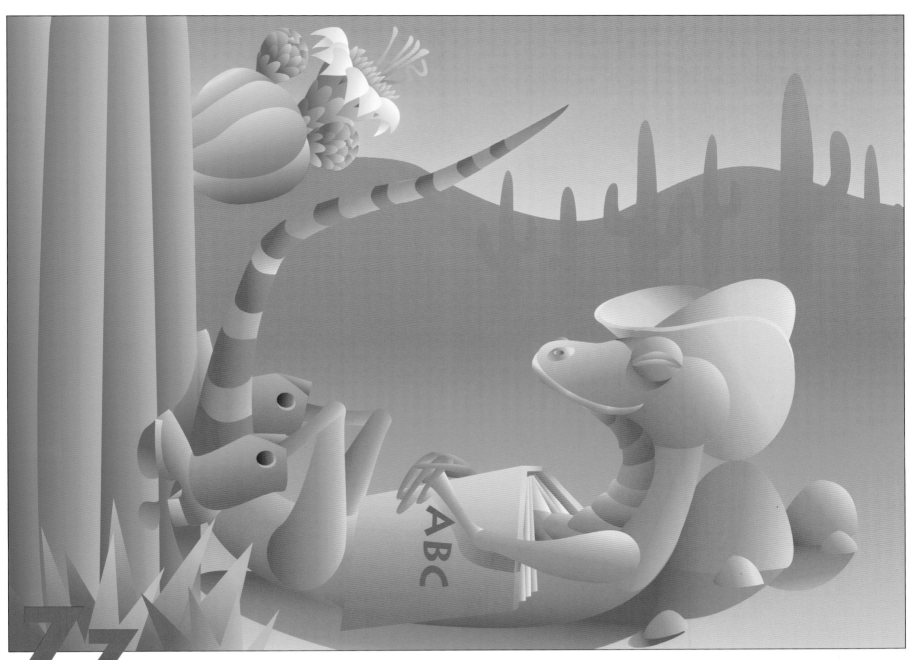

Z Z Z

Zebratail lizard

Zeb Zebratail is catching some ZZZs and dreaming of his ABCs.

"Z" should be no problem to find. If you think it's on the saguaro flower, you're reading my mind.

GLOSSARY

Alamo: A big fort and church in Texas where people like Davey Crockett and Jim Bowie fought in a war against Mexico more than 100 years ago.

Armadillo: A small animal that has a hard armor-like shell over its body and head. It sleeps during the day and comes out at night. It likes to eat bugs.

Barrel Cactus: A round cactus that has yellow, red, or orange flowers. It grows yellow fruit that tastes good.

Buffalo: A brown, furry, cowlike animal with short horns. It is as tall as a person and weighs as much as a pickup truck.

Coyote: A small fast animal that looks like a medium-size dog with a long pointed nose.

28

Dinosaur: A big lizardlike animal that lived a long time ago. Some dinosaurs were as small as a dog, and some were bigger than a building.

Elf Owl: This is the smallest owl in the United States. It eats bugs and lives in a saguaro cactus.

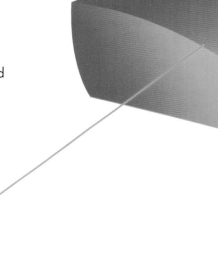

Fox: A small animal related to the dog. It weighs about as much as a family cat, and can live up to 14 years.

Gecko: A small, harmless lizard that lives where it's warm and eats bugs. It has a short, flat, bumpy body, and likes to walk upside down.

Grand Canyon: Our country's greatest canyon. It is located in Arizona and has rocks almost 2 billion years old. The Colorado River made the canyon a long, long, time ago. A lot of animals and birds live there.

Horned Toad: A small, gentle lizard that looks mean, but isn't. It is small enough to hold in your hand, and has spines on its head, sides, and back. It can "spit" blood from its eyes when it is scared.

Ibis: A big bird that lives where it is warm and where there is water. It has a long neck, long legs, and a long bill. It eats bugs, fish, and frogs.

Jackalope: A make-believe animal that looks like a big rabbit with antlers.

Kangaroo Rat: A little rat that is 4 inches tall with a tail that is 5 inches long. It sleeps during the day and plays at night. It eats seeds and never has to drink water in its whole life.

Lake Powell: A great big man-made lake that holds 9 trillion gallons of water.

Monument Valley: A large valley where many Navajo Indians live. Cowboy movies are made there.

Mountain Lion: A huge, wild cat that purrs like a house cat. It usually sleeps during the day and comes out at night.

GLOSSARY

Ocotillo: A different looking plant that has long, green stems and pretty flowers that are shaped like red tubes and are filled with a sweet liquid called nectar. Hummingbirds and bees like to come to the plant to eat the nectar.

Ocelot: A medium-size wild cat that has spots on its coat. It lives mainly in the forests of the Southwest.

Painted Desert: A pretty desert where the sun shining on the rocks shows colors of reds, oranges, grays, blues, purples, yellows, and whites.

Peccary: This wild animal is also called a javelina. It looks like a hairy pig with tusks. It likes to eat plants, even cactus, spines and all.

Prickly Pear Cactus: A common cactus that stores water. It has yellow, purple, white, or cream-colored flowers that can be eaten. People make candy and jelly from its red fruit.

Quail: A bird that lives in the desert. It has a fat body and a dark, small feather that sticks up on top of its head.

Rattlesnake: A snake that can hurt you if it bites you. Rattlesnakes cannot hear and are poisonous, so they should not be touched or picked up.

Roadrunner: A bird that loves to run very fast instead of fly, but it can fly if it needs to. The roadrunner likes to eat bugs, snakes, and lizards.

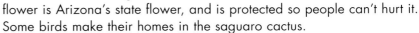

Saguaro Cactus: This is the biggest cactus in the United States. It only grows in some Southwest deserts. It has white flowers that bloom at night and fruit that can be eaten. The saguaro cactus flower is Arizona's state flower, and is protected so people can't hurt it. Some birds make their homes in the saguaro cactus.

Sunset Crater: A large cinder cone that was made a long time ago when a volcano erupted. It is in northern Arizona near Flagstaff.

Tortoise: A turtle that lives only on land and not in the water. It lives in holes in the ground to keep cool, and it eats plants. Some tortoises have lived for more than 100 years.

Unicorn: A pretend animal that looks like a white horse with a long horn in the middle of its forehead.

Vulture: A large bird that cannot make any noise, except for small hisses. It can see and fly very well, and it keeps its feathers very clean.

Wildcat: A medium-size cat that is also called a bobcat because it has a really short tail. It is shy and hides from people, hunting at night for rats and mice to eat.

Yellow Warbler: This is a small bright-yellow bird. It eats insects off leaves and twigs of trees and plants.

Yellowstone National Park: This is our oldest national park and it is very big, going through three different states: Wyoming, Idaho, and Montana.

Zebratail Lizard: This is the fastest lizard. When it runs, its long tail curls and shows its tail stripes. It likes to live in dry, open areas like the desert.